Kirk Caudle

Joseph Smith and the United States Presidency

Delusions of Grandeur or Genuine Ambitions?

GRIN Publishing

Bibliographic information published by the German National Library:

The German National Library lists this publication in the National Bibliography; detailed bibliographic data are available on the Internet at http://dnb.dnb.de .

Imprint:

Copyright © 2010 GRIN Verlag, Open Publishing GmbH
Print and binding: Books on Demand GmbH, Norderstedt Germany
ISBN: 978-3-640-78063-1

This book at GRIN:

http://www.grin.com/en/e-book/155926/joseph-smith-and-the-united-states-presidency

GRIN - Your knowledge has value

Since its foundation in 1998, GRIN has specialized in publishing academic texts by students, college teachers and other academics as e-book and printed book. The website www.grin.com is an ideal platform for presenting term papers, final papers, scientific essays, dissertations and specialist books.

Visit us on the internet:

http://www.grin.com/

http://www.facebook.com/grincom

http://www.twitter.com/grin_com

Kirk Caudle

Marylhurst University

Southwest Texas Popular Culture and American Culture Conference

10-13 February 2010

Joseph Smith and the Presidency: Delusions of Grandeur or Genuine Ambitions?

Joseph Smith started more than a religion; he led a political cultural movement that is still a force in contemporary American politics. One need look no further than the 2008 Republican Presidential nominate Mitt Romney or the Senate Majority leader, Democrat Harry Reid.[1] Until recently, serious scholarship on the impact of Joseph Smith's political aspirations has been lacking. Former studies of the life of Joseph Smith often contain half-truths and attempts to desecrate his character while giving little credit to the larger role he plays in the history of American politics and religion. A closer look inside his candidacy rejects personal power claims. It instead points to sincere motives to provide protection and religious freedom for all oppressed Untied States citizens by increasing the power of the federal government, and installing righteous leaders to assure that protection is realized. While this does not prove him to be a prophet, it nonetheless solidifies his places in American political history.

Joseph Smith functioned as both prophet and president of the Church of Jesus Christ of Latter-day Saints.[2] After the establishment of the Church in 1830, persecution continuously plagued the Saints. This was no more evident than when Missouri Governor Liburn Boggs issued his infamous "Mormon Extermination order" on 27 October 1838. Here, Governor Boggs attempted a sort of "ethnic cleansing" to expel the Mormons from his state. Mormon leadership exercised futile attempts to rescind the order, but with fatal results (Hartley 10-11). However, during this time it was not uncommon for the United States government to dismiss cultures they did not agree with or understand. An example of this can be seen in President Andrew Jackson's deplorable treatment of the Native Americans in 1830 (Hartley 5-7). This was a hard time to be an ethnic or religious minority in the United States.

Missourians disagreed with Mormon theology, but they feared Mormon politics. The Mormons quickly became a majority in counties they settled in by purchasing previously unoccupied land. Inevitably political disagreements turned to violence. This was the case at one polling station during August 1838 when the Mormon majority was refused the right to vote in Davies County, Missouri (Abanes 156-57, 188-89). Mobs, fearful of the Mormon political influence, often tortured both Joseph Smith and his followers by the means of tar and feathering (Bushman 225-27). These violent mobs formed to intimidate the Saints, prevent them from voting, and ultimately from living in their own homes.

Feeling the civil rights of his followers was infringed upon, Joseph Smith traveled to Washington to appeal to President Martin Van Buren. Although leery of politicians, Joseph Smith had faith that the power contained in the United States Constitution would save his people. However, he found the exact opposite to be true upon his arrival. While pleading his case before the president he was told, "your cause is just, but I can do nothing for you," because if he acted he would "lose the vote of Missouri" (Roberts 4: 80). Such a blatant political power play disgusted Joseph Smith. As he left Washington he stated, "May he [Van Buren] never be elected again to any office of trust or power" (Roberts 4: 89). Whatever faith Joseph Smith carried into the meeting regarding the United States governing powers to address the needs of his people had vanished. After this encounter, one might conclude that in the mind of Joseph Smith, the secular government of the United States was now not only his enemy, but God's enemy.

With few friends and few places to turn, the Saints went north to Illinois where they found refuge in a town named Commerce, in Hancock County. After settling here, the Mormons renamed the town Nauvoo. Joseph Smith said the name Nauvoo was "of Hebrew origin, and signifies a beautiful situation, or place, carrying with it, also, the idea of rest; and is truly descriptive of the most delightful location" (Roberts 4: 268; Smith 182). However, Joseph Smith and his people found only brief solace in Nauvoo before the Missouri mobs again tried to take his life and imprison him. The reason most often cited for his arrest was on the basis of treason, although scholars debate the legitimacy of these claims.[3] He faced extradition not only from a state government, but even from within his own inner circle of believers as he was "technically a fugitive from justice" (Bushman 426).

During this period in Nauvoo, apostasy became common place among church members, many of whom were converts from Protestant Christianity. Joseph Smith claimed many new revelations that these former Protestants saw as a great departure from their own personal religious views, and felt they could no longer support the prophet in his efforts. Historian Timothy Wood observed, 'the new body of doctrine alienated many Mormons . . . the new revelations concerning multiple marriage . . . plurality of god, and eternal human progression, precipitated a large departure from the church during the last year of Smith's life" (188). Of the issues listed by Wood, Protestant converts might have had the hardest time dealing with the doctrine of polygamy.

Polygamy came alive as a significant, and divisive, issue within Mormonism during this time in Nauvoo. In 1842, Joseph Smith and other select church members became involved in the practice (Leonard 345-46). However, not all Mormon leaders agreed with Joseph Smith on the issue of polygamy, including Sidney Rigdon, who would become his Presidential running mate. Many leaders saw the doctrine of plural marriage as "inconstant with previously revealed doctrine" (Leonard 348). Most of who disputed Joseph Smith on this doctrine either left the church or were excommunicated (ibid). These events caused Joseph Smith to feel pressure as a prophet losing the faith of his followers. This also placed him in the predicament of trying to lead these same people as a statesman.

However, Joseph Smith's next move revealed he was "never passive" when it came to politics (Ostling and Ostling 3). After repeated failed attempts at federal government protection for himself, and the people he led, Joseph Smith became disillusioned with both parties. This disillusionment motivated him to appoint himself as an independent candidate for the United States presidency in 1844, with friend and confidant Sidney Rigdon as his running mate (Roberts 6:210-11). Joseph Smith led the Saints to Nauvoo in 1839, seeking religious freedom and the rights of the members of his church to worship as they pleased without living in continual fear of the violent mobs.

Joseph Smith felt he must run for president because no other politician would defend the constitutional rights of his people (Roberts 4: 188,243). He felt all citizens had inalienable rights which the United States government no longer protected. Besides the practical reason of physical protection, Joseph Smith believed the Constitution was a document divinely inspired by God himself that "should be maintained for the rights and protection of all flesh, according to just and holy principles (Doctrine and Covenants 101.77-78).[4] As God's prophet on the earth he felt a political obligation to see to its protection. To do this in the name of God seems foreign in the twenty first century, but in the context of the nineteenth century it was much more commonplace. Joseph Smith lived in a century of "dreamlike politics" (Bushman 521). This was not only in the United States, but around the world. Richard Bushman remarked "Marx dreamed of government withering away. Dostoevsky envisioned a theocratic kingdom of God on earth . . . revolutions tore up most of Europe in 1848. In the United States, the issue of God in government was still alive . . . from a certain Christian prospective government under God was logical and natural" (521-22).

Joseph Smith laid out his political platform in an essay titled, *Views of the Power and Policy of the Government of the United States* (hereafter referred to as *Views*)[5]. This "was generally considered an impressive document" (Robertson 149-150). *Views* included, but was not limited to, commentary on the annexation of Texas, expanding the power of the federal government, and slavery. *Views* contained references from every United States president with the exception of Martin Van Buren, on whom Joseph Smith blamed the majority of the Nation's problems (Wood 176-180). Richard Bushman saw Joseph Smith "driven by political expediency" which in turn "had made himself into a son of America" (513). Joseph wanted to paint a picture of himself as a real American, not just a Mormon. However, many non-Mormons saw a fraudulent prophet and therefore viewed his rationale with the utmost skepticism.

The logical question now arises, why did those living in the United States during the 1830's and 40's fear the Mormons? The problems Joseph Smith faced as a Presidential candidate might not be so different than those that Mormon candidates face today. When a PBS interviewer asked Utah Historian, Ken Verdoia, what people in Joseph Smith's day found "so startling and upsetting" to the people, he responded:

> If you look at the way local newspapers that are not affiliated with Joseph Smith and the Mormons look at the Mormons, they are aghast at the perfect union of church and political leadership that exists in that community. Joseph Smith is absolute authority for all things religious and all things political and all things economic and all things social. Now, that is discordant with what a lot of these new Americans believe about the nation . . . That troubles the newspaper editors; it troubles the local mayors; it troubles state legislators; it troubles governors. It even troubles Washington, D.C. (para. 6)

Joseph Smith's assailants accused him of being a power hungry dictator and a megalomaniac. Many believed he ran for President so he could build his own Mormon Kingdom within the United States (Brodie 285-86). Some even supposed he ultimately imaged naming himself not only as king over the nation, but the entire world (Abanes 189). The basis for these claims often grew from statements made by Joseph Smith. Among these came in 1831 (over a decade before his campaign) when he declared that Independence, Missouri was "appointed and consecrated for the gathering of the saints" and was "the land of promise, and the place for the city of Zion" while the center of the city was to include a Temple for Mormon worship (Doctrine and Covenants 57.1-4). Fawn Brodie shares a common vantage point with many when she stated in her unflattering biography that, "Joseph was now fully intoxicated with power and drunk with visions of empire and apocalyptic glory. After referring to God as his "right hand man" Brodie believes he was having what "sober men would have called delusions of grandeur" (354).

Antagonists felt that Joseph Smith had already seized too much power in Illinois, and especially in Nauvoo itself. He was not only the Mayor of Nauvoo, but also the leader of the Nauvoo Legion military force, and owned the largest store in the town. Brodie observed Joseph Smith as nothing more than a great speaker with a personality people naturally wanted to follow and that, "the source of his power lay not in his doctrine but in his person" (ix). Richard Abanes, author of *One Nation Under Gods* and expert on the occult, observed, "intellectual reasoning and logical thought never had played more than a minor role in [his] belief system" (176). The non-Mormons in the area found it particularly unsettling that Joseph Smith petitioned Congress in mid-1843 to raise a 100,000 man army under his control. Citizens became anxious as this would be in addition to the "Lieutenant-General Joseph Smith" led Nauvoo Legion, which during 1844 was half the size of the entire army of the United States (Abanes 182-33). This added to the public's impression of him as a self-centered and narcissistic religious fanatic.

Joseph Smith retaliated with a political platform, not simply with theology. The presidential campaign put together a group of no less than 340 electioneers that went across the United States distributing copies of his essay, *Views* (Robertson 147). However, no matter how far away from Missouri these electioneers advanced on the campaign trail; they still ran into mob troubles at times. Because of differences in religious beliefs, it was not uncommon for death threats to be leveled against Joseph Smith, especially in the south. Although, "on the whole, the electioneers did not record a violent or rowdy campaign" (Robertson 150-151). The troubles experienced by the electioneers underscore the problems Joseph Smith saw in the United States: religious freedom and tolerance.

A primary duty of the government, Joseph Smith surmised, was to let religions grow. He challenged any political party that impeded advancement from occurring. He regularly quoted the Founding Fathers on the "inalienable rights" of man. In an official statement to the church he said:

The Declaration of Independence 'holds these truths to be self-evident, that all men are created equal: that they are endowed by their Creator with certain inalienable rights; that among these are life, liberty, and the pursuit of happiness,' but, at the same time, some two or three millions of people are held as slaves for life, because the spirit in them is covered with a darker skin than ours . . . The Constitution of the United States of America meant just what it said without reference to color or condition, ad infinitum! (Clark 1:191-2)

The free agency of mankind is a hallmark of the Mormon faith, and was a theological view carried into the campaign. Joseph Smith saw the current state of agency as deficient and the government's efforts to fix the problem severely inadequate. As previously stated in this essay, Joseph Smith campaigned on the major issues of his time: a stronger (although smaller) federal government, slavery, and Texas. These issues all advanced his goal of providing agency for all Americans.

Because of his strong belief in the right of agency for every person, Joseph Smith lobbied for a strong federal government that had the power to step in when a state had over-stepped its bounds in taking away the rights of an individual (Busman 512-17). Troubles in Missouri, where his followers became the subjects of abuse in the name of state rights, appear to have jaded him. Two weeks prior to announcing his candidacy, Joseph Smith referred to state rights as a doctrine that "fed mobs" and "shall ascend up as a stink offering in the nose of the Almighty" (qtd. in Bushman 514).

Joseph Smith set forth an idea to rid the nation from slavery by 1850. He purposed to offer slave owners money to give up their slaves after sale of public land. However, he was not a staunch abolitionist and never advocated for the immediate release of all slaves (Wood 180-181), although he also claimed that they came into "the world slaves, mentally and physically. Change their situation with the whites, and they would be like them. They have souls and are subject to salvation. Go to Cincinnati or any city, and find an educated Negro, who rides in his carriage, and you will see a man who has risen by his own mind to his exalted state of respectability" (Roberts 5: 217). Joseph Smith saw the Mormons entrenched in a similar situation as the slaves and the Indians.

To remedy the slavery situation, Joseph Smith campaigned in favor of annexing Texas into the Union. However, although he was an expansionist, he did not want to expand simply for the sake of expansion. He wanted Texas to be a free state. On 7 March 1844 Joseph Smith said, "It will be more honorable for us to receive Texas and set the negroes free, and use the negroes and Indians against our foes." But Joseph Smith did not want to stop with Texas. "The South holds the balance of power. By annexing Texas, I can do away with this evil. As soon as Texas was annexed, I would liberate the negroes to Texas, and from Texas to Mexico, where all colors are alike. And if that was not sufficient, I would call upon Canada, and annex it" (Roberts 6: 243-44). Therefore, from this perspective, one might suppose Joseph Smith set out to release a nation from under the bondage of a government that suppressed the religious and inalienable rights of its citizens.

Joseph Smith assured these same religious, and inalienable, rights were afforded to the citizens in Nauvoo. In fact, Nauvoo itself was a hub of religious freedom and tolerance. As Mayor, Joseph Smith believed every citizen possessed the right to worship as they pleased, even if he personally disagreed. "Every man has a natural, and, in our country, a constitutional right to be a false prophet, as well as a true prophet" (Smith 357). Although religious freedom was present, the opponents of Joseph Smith still doubted the sincerity, and reality, of these claims. Many believed the proof of how the Mormons really felt about outsiders presented themselves when Mormons voted for common candidates and policies (Abanes 187-90). As this was an issue in Missouri, Mormons voting together again became a hotly contested point of contention in Illinois.

The Mormons did indeed often vote in league with one another. They presented themselves almost as a must win for any candidate running for office in Illinois during the 1840's, boasting a voting population of at least 40,000 people (Abanes 189). However, an understanding of free agency within Nauvoo, and to an extent within the Church itself, is essential to understanding the purpose of why the Mormons voted as a bloc, while they were often accused of blindly following of a false prophet. The Mormons voting for common candidates could be perceived as a lack of religious freedom, even from within their own communities. However, Joseph Smith claims he never told his followers what candidate to vote for during elections. He provided the following reasoning:

> I will show you how we have been situated by bringing a comparison. Should there be a Methodist society here and two candidates running for office, one says, 'If you will vote for me and put me in as governor, I will exterminate the Methodists, take away their charters,' etc. The other candidate says, 'If I am governor, I will give all an equal privilege.' Which would the Methodists vote for? Of course they would vote EN MASSE for the candidate that would give them their rights. Thus it has been with us (Roberts 5: 490)

Thus, accusing the Mormons of voting in unison because of a common theological view, or blindly following Joseph Smith, is over simplifying the situation.

The Mormons possessed practicable reasons for voting together. They voted for the protection of their families, themselves, their friends, and their religious freedom. Mormons voted for similar policies because it was often times the only logical conclusion to which one in their position could come. However, Joseph Smith made clear to his followers that he did not claim prophetic revelation on political matters. Any ideas he put forth were his own, and as previously stated, Joseph Smith did not command the Church to vote for one candidate over another (Roberts 5: 526).

During the campaign, Joseph Smith always kept one eye on Washington and the other on the western frontier. While it is a fact Joseph Smith asked to raise an "Army of the West" he did not do so to protect his own life, but in the spirit of his campaign, to protect emigrants moving west to Oregon country seeking religious freedom. During this era emigrants moving westward faced dangers from robbers and Indians. In fact, this army would have no jurisdiction outside of the western frontier and was the brainchild of Benjamin Franklin. Franklin imagined people "settling the west" under the protection of "civilian militias." This army also, according to Franklin, would serve to promote the freedom of movement and ideas (Bushman 571-22).

Joseph Smith was taken into custody after destroying the inaugural issue of the *Nauvoo Expositor* newspaper in June of 1844. The events surrounding this event became engulfed in political controversy, as did his murder by the hands of a military organization from Missouri while in jail in for the destruction of the *Expositor*. Some modern scholars now believe his assailants killed him with government issued weapons (Lyon and Lyon 7). This obviously assured Joseph Smith never made it to the election (Doctrine and Covenants 135). The *Expositor* accused Joseph Smith of everything from adultery to perjury. In his book, *One Nation Under Gods*, Richard Abanes absurdly claims that Joseph Smith destroyed the Newspaper because it threatened to undercover his plan to "rule the world" (545n122). This is a blatant anti-Mormon claim that has carries no legitimacy. It appears more likely that Joseph Smith, acting as Mayor, felt the newspaper threatened the security of the city. He described the paper as "a public nuisance" and called for the printing press to be destroyed "without delay." City officials carried out the order (Roberts 6:432-49). After a fourteen year struggle—since 1830—the mobs finally caught up with Joseph Smith.

Nineteenth century Mormon leaders believed the martyrdom of Joseph Smith, their prophet, carried both great spiritual and political ramifications. At the forefront of these was the American Civil War. It was common for Mormon leaders to preach about the rejection of God in relation to the death of Joseph Smith as a reason for the War Between the States (Noll 80-81). Therefore, the presidential candidacy of Joseph Smith meant more to the Saints than simply winning an election. It meant keeping God on the side of America.

Whether or not Joseph Smith was a legitimate contender for the Presidential seat is debatable, and has been widely discussed elsewhere. However, those that campaigned for him campaigned as if he would win, even though Joseph Smith himself stated, "I care little for the Presidential chair" (Roberts 6: 243). As it has been shown throughout this essay, he cared more for the welfare of the church and the nation than he did his own personal achievements. This could be one possible why reason his electioneers trusted him with the welfare of the nation. Margaret Robertson presents an antithetical from that of Fawn Brodie, while remarking that "the electioneers . . . presenting his [Joseph Smiths] *Views* and his name to the people of the United States is evidence neither that the Prophet was a megalomaniac nor that he was grasping for power or secretly planning to take over the government. It is evidence merely that he was running for president" (164-65). The political campaign of Joseph Smith proved not to be inconstant with other campaigns of the time. This was shown though the political activities of the electioneers who expressed faith in the vision of Joseph Smith for the United States.

In modern times, The Church of Jesus Christ of Latter-day Saints distinguishes itself from other Christian religious movements in the United States, "as one of the fastest growing religious denominations" in the country (Wood 167). In the nineteenth century, controversy followed the movement's founder, Joseph Smith, throughout his life. This essay has shown views on the character and sanity of Joseph Smith shift from one extreme to the other. However, whether one views Joseph Smith as "a great impostor, or a great visionary" it cannot be denied he is "one of the most remarkable persons who has appeared on the stage of the world in modern times" (qtd. in Bancroft and Bates 464).

Although not widely discussed today, perhaps few decisions received more scrutiny from his enemies than his declaration to contend for the 1844 presidential seat. With his true motives continually questioned, he explored options to bring legitimacy to his campaign. His run at the United States presidency was more than a political stunt, as he possessed sincere political aspirations for the protection of all oppressed peoples. As the membership of Mormonism continues to rise throughout the world, historians, politicians, and theologians would benefit from understanding the political roots of this faith as they continue to be a force in societies at large. This essay also provides a starting point for further study on the impact of Joseph Smith, the politician, on contemporary Mormon policies and politics in the world. In spite of charges to the contrary, Joseph Smith does not just have a place in American religious history, but has a concrete place in the history of American politics. Therefore, Mormons, and non-Mormons alike, can benefit from a better understanding of his political endeavors.

Notes

---

[1] For an in-depth look at Mormons in contemporary politics which is outside the scope of this essay, see Ostling and Ostling, esp 82-86.

[2] Members of the Church of Jesus Christ of Latter-day Saints are most commonly referred to as "Mormons." However, other appropriate nicknames include the abbreviation LDS (as in Latter-day Saints) or simply "The Saints." These names are employed in this essay.

[3] Bushman provides an extensive look at Joseph Smith's various imprisonments during his lifetime (373-390).

[4] Mormons believe *The Doctrine and Covenants* contain a compellation of revelations given to Joseph Smith and other church leaders between 1838 and 1978. *The Doctrine and Covenants* is included in the Mormon canon of scripture.

[5] This document is also sometimes referred to as *General Smith's Views of the Powers and Policy of the Government of the United States*, which became the official name after its publication. However, Roberts refers to it by the name used in this essay.